Success in English for the 11+

A Guide for Parents and Tutors

© Stuart Riddle

ISBN13:9781546449867
ISBN-10:1546449868

Published in 2017 by White Rabbit Publishing

London N1

Published in the United Kingdom.

SUCCESS IN THE 11+: A GUIDE FOR PARENTS AND TUTORS

STUART RIDDLE

White Rabbit
Publications

ACKNOWLEDGEMENTS

Heartfelt thanks to Raj whose idea to write this book was, Lynne Fox for proofreading with exactitude and helpful suggestions; and Jan Carmichael who ran with the idea, did all the typing, editing, layout and without whom this work would not have seen the light of day.

TABLE OF CONTENTS

*All unattributed quotations are taken from the
works of Lewis Carroll*

"and what is the use of a book",
thought Alice, "without pictures
or conversation?"

FOREWORD

Many parents feel understandably nervous when faced with the prospect of their child taking the 11+ or Common Entrance examination and want to help their child but don't really know where to start. This guide will help you to negotiate the wealth of information available and offers pointers to resources that have stood the test of time, as well as showing you how to teach your child the finer points of English which are so vital to a good result. Several parents have seen the results of my teaching and urged me to write this guide as they felt it would be helpful to parents who either do not want or are unable to employ a home tutor for one reason or another.

It will also be of use to people who do employ a tutor but also want to add to it by undertaking some extra tuition themselves. I have therefore explained *how* I teach and *what* I teach in detail.

I cannot guarantee your child will pass the exam because, as well as a good teacher, this depends on the ability of the individual child, but I can guarantee that if you use the methods outlined in this text, your child will, at the very least, raise the marks they would have obtained without tuition.

I sincerely hope you find this guide is useful to you and your child and wish you both the best of luck!

Stuart Riddle

August 2017

INTRODUCTION

This guide is designed for the dedicated and devoted parent who wishes to help their child to attain a coveted place in a private or grammar school at age 11. The focus is mostly on the English part of the examination. It may also be of help to the professional or trainee tutor.

Parents need to do their research well in advance to find a list of appropriate schools and discover the exact nature of their respective entrance exams, as well as finding out such facts as journey time to school, and alternative schools; whether school buses are available; cost etc. Lots of information can be gleaned from the internet, parents' chat rooms and forums etc about "issues" with various schools, as well as talking to parents you already know. Detailed planning can often take place two years in advance of the examination. Many pupils begin preparation in Year 4, mostly on basic skills and the pressure intensifies in Year 5, building to a point of intensity a month or two before the examinations are taken.

This book is divided into three parts:

Part I deals in detail with my teaching methods and how to proceed with teaching writing and learning for both Years 4 and Year 5.

Part II deals with elements of grammar and vocabulary and the best way to teach this.

Part III contains various example comprehension exercises, a sample lesson plan and a list of resources which have been an invaluable aid to me during my time as a tutor. They are all easily available and the list is up-to-date. It does not attempt to be a complete list, as there are many resources available for the 11+; it is a list of tried and trusted materials that are available and will not overwhelm the parent/tutor with volume and variety. The focus has been on quality.

THE 11+

The 11+ is not a straightforward examination. In contrast to most other examinations, there is no one way to prepare for it and obviously it is not taught and therefore does not entail revision. Indeed, there is only one chance and no re-sits ! This "one chance only" is lessened, to an extent, by parents applying to three, four or five schools at the same time and the child sitting all the exams as an insurance in attaining at least one place if they cannot get into their school of choice. This strategy may include grammar schools and fee-paying schools. It is therefore a tough examination and pupils (and parents!) face it with some trepidation, which is quite understandable. Some of the parents reading this will never have sat the exam themselves and have no prior knowledge of it. Others will remember taking it and the general anxiety with which they attempted it. Some will have been prepared by their school, but others will not. Many schools believe that the examination cannot be prepared for but this is patently untrue as the following text will demonstrate.

When I first take on a pupil, I find out what their strengths and weaknesses are and cover the ground where I find weaknesses with particular care. The weaknesses I usually find are:

- Lack of grammar or the need to tighten up on basic grammar.
- Not enough paragraphs, or indeed, no paragraphs at all! Continuous rambling prose, which makes the writing boring and tedious.
- Words missing from context or syntax. This is often due to not reading through what has been written at the end of the examination, so the prose is uneven and almost unintelligible.
- Poor spelling in some areas of vocabulary (for example, "wich" for "which").
- Some level of dyslexia which means systematic and continually poor spelling.
- Poor and repetitive vocabulary which makes the writing "flat".

Practice over a few months can address these various weaknesses. A weekly writing session where work is corrected can give a great boost to skills as well as confidence. Almost all pupils have one or more of these weaknesses in their prose and writing but at age 10, pupils learn quickly and most issues are readily addressed.

PART I

TEACHING AND WRITING: DEVELOPMENT FROM YEAR 4

How to begin tutoring

I am usually engaged to tutor for an hour per week although sometimes this can go up to two, three or even four hours in the weeks or months leading up to the examination. This is only one layer of input because many parents won't be able to afford this or indeed, may wish to tutor their child individually at home which can be more testing because of the close emotional relationship. Parents often tell me that they cannot work with their children. Perhaps 'cannot' is too strong a word, but the fact remains that some children do not respond to close tuition from parents and learn as they would from a stranger. A common complaint from mothers is "my kids won't listen to me". This is nothing to do with intelligence or capacity to learn, it is an issue of motivation and the "professional stranger" sometimes has more success in this area. Nevertheless, many parents do have great success. e.g. often the parent has great success in tutoring mathematics to the child. This can complement a tutor's English specialism. Two of the main issues here are that of temperament and personality and the dynamics of the home environment. What are the boundaries and expectations of the child? What do the parents expect?

Tutoring ideally begins 12 – 15 months prior to sitting an examination. This may be from the end of Year 4 right the way through Year 5. I always begin as I mean to go on; to use a somewhat tired cliché. Some parents think an hour is too long but in fact, this is part of the training, because pupils need to focus for an hour or an hour and half for the examination in English. Endurance is required, an endurance to which they are not exposed in the schoolroom. Tuition can be quite relaxed but also intense and there is no escape in a one-to-one setting. To begin, I always insist on the title and date being written out in full so there can be evidence of clear progression and to encourage good habits. I always teach, for the most part, from a comprehension passage. There are many available books to be purchased in educational outlets, or on line for example, giving passages which suit this purpose. I use both the Nelson and the Schofield & Simms series, which are age-related. A short passage is read, either by the tutor or the pupil, or often by taking turns with each paragraph. Language is explained and things pointed out such as similes, metaphors etc. It is in reading passages such as this that you can assess the competence of the pupil as to whether the language, grammar and content are too easy or too difficult. When asked this, children often respond by saying "it's in the middle" which I have learned to take as a good sign that we are both addressing the right level. Passages are usually extracts from books, many of which are quite intriguing and pupils should be encouraged to research more about them or even read the books in their entirety. Some pupils may be enthusiastic to read more of "The Hobbit" or "Kidnapped" after being exposed to one or two pages of the original text.

There are questions to answer, up to a dozen, all with varying degrees of difficulty. The authors of the text have usually designed the questions to run sequentially through the paragraphs. Pupils must be told this and reminded at each session, as this helps them in searching for answers. Usually, new pupils will guess or think they know the answer to even the simplest question but they must be trained to refer back to the text and read the relevant section. This is of great importance because guessing the answer usually means that they get it contextually wrong. If they get stuck I always narrow things down to say that the answer is in "this particular paragraph" (say paragraph 2), or even to count or narrow the search down to one or two lines so that the pupil may uncover the answer themselves, (say line 17 and 18) but pupils are always amazed that I have counted down the lines to give them an accurate pointer.

I always require answers to be written out in full sentences, unless "the paper" dictates otherwise; children aged 8 and 9 are prone to giving monosyllabic responses but I always include the beginning of the question in the answer.

A large rose-tree stood near the entrance of the garden: the roses growing on it were white, but there were three gardeners at it, busily painting them red. Alice thought this a very curious thing, and she went nearer to watch them, and just as she came up to them she heard one of them say 'Look out now, Five! Don't go splashing paint over me like that!'

'I couldn't help it,' said Five, in a sulky tone: 'Seven jogged my elbow'.

On which Seven looked up and said 'That's right, Five! Always lay the blame on others!'

For example, referring to this passage from Alice in Wonderland, (at the beginning of Chapter 8), I might ask the question 'What

15

were the gardeners doing?' the question being worth two marks. A response could be 'the gardeners were painting white roses red' and a fuller response could include the fact that the gardeners were arguing. This full exposition of the question helps clarity of thought and clarity of execution. I sometimes give half of a sentence on paper so that the pupil may complete the rest of the question. This is training both in good habits and 'sequencing' because often the exact wording of a question will be forgotten and hence misinterpreted (even slightly). Rereading the question is important here and requires some attention because the question may have several parts and must be answered fully to attain full marks. Note: the gardeners are painting and arguing.

Reading the Question

To develop this idea further, we might include the phrase 'in your own words explain what the gardeners were doing' (four marks). To do this properly is not easy and pupils often forget the prefix 'in your own words', and answer the question in language from the text. A useful response might be 'the workers were colouring/staining the blooms a different colour' (this is very difficult and may require a lot of thought), notably, substituting language for the words "painting" and "flowers". In addition, the gardeners/workers were arguing as well and this point may be forgotten.

Again, personally, I need to read the question several times to confirm that I have fully understood it myself and the pupil should be trained to do this too. I realise this might be stating the obvious, but it is a technique that must be mastered to obtain a good result in the examination. Questions are deliberately set out in this way to differentiate between pupils and until properly trained, seven out of ten children will only give a partial response to a question of this nature and will not obtain full marks. Competition is intense in these types of examinations (up to one place given for every 20 applicants at some schools in London,) so careful systematic skills need to be gently fostered in understanding the question.

The Value of Questions

Some questions require much more work than others. This is a significant point. How do we know which questions need more work? Ninety percent of examination papers carry marks at the end of each question so that we know how the questions are loaded. Thus, six mark questions will need three times as much commentary as a two mark question. Each school is different but the pupil must be trained to look and to look carefully. A paper which gives one mark for the opening questions for a simple answer and then poses a question for two marks will require two points of evidence or an extended answer to a question in order to attain the best grade. This must be trained into the pupil from the very beginning, even before practice examination papers are attempted. Primary school children are sometimes resistant to writing a lot or even in full sentences and try to escape by producing a minimalist answer. This cannot be allowed and the pupil and tutor must labour to find more points to respond to. This is vital to attain full marks in the examination. The whole thrust of detailed tutoring work is to provide high quality responses.

Grammar and Timing

In the beginning, at the end of Year 4 and the initial stages of Year 5 there should be no focus on time constraints. Answers must be given as full, complete and exact. This is not as difficult as it sounds. Content is provided by the text that you are reading and grammatical corrections made as the pupil goes along, for example, capitals, full stops, commas, spelling errors, errors of tense, and the insertion of missing words. Intuition may be used in providing more advanced grammar than many pupils have been exposed to. Children will respond to learning and embrace it if they are motivated. For example, I recently had a seven year old who was happy to use the colon correctly in making lists. So if appropriate, I do try to introduce slowly more sophisticated grammar, such as the use of brackets and the ellipses which occur almost organically and flow naturally from tuition, not imposed from above. Pupils naturally enjoy extending their knowledge and skills in this area because they know they are learning and doing well.

Continually praise pupils. This is a standard technique, the formula being, to give three lots of praise, balanced by one of criticism. No one wants to have their work criticised all the time, so as you correct with a pen the errors of the last sentence, you make positive statements about what they have done, whilst pointing out the minor issue of e.g. "this word is not spelt correctly" or "what punctuation do we need here?" etc. Lots of praise and encouragement is vital for self-confidence. Generally, I tell pupils not to be afraid to make mistakes because this is how they are going to learn. Similarly, "Don't be afraid to ask for help; I won't be sitting next to you in the examination".

As well as this, I always encourage pupils to lead where appropriate e.g. "Which bit of work do you want to do?" Give choices. To give them choices means they are more in control. Praise is a vital tool in building confidence.

To summarise the key points covered so far:

- Importance of the value of questions
- Grammar learning in Year 4
- Give praise
- Answer the question fully

DEVELOPMENT IN YEAR 5

During Year 5, at an appropriate point to be judged by the tutor, usually after about three months' tuition, we will move on to undertaking past 11+ papers and comprehension passages. I use papers from a variety of sources, and of differing lengths and qualities. Thus, we introduce grammar gradually, as it arises. There can be problems of syntax such as the tenses of verbs or the use of the definite article ("the"). This can happen a lot with pupils whose first language is not English.

Regarding grammar, basic grammar is comprised of the use of capital letters, commas, the apostrophe, full stop and exclamation marks where appropriate. The apostrophe must be mastered both in its singular and plural form and as a contraction. Any good grammar text with worked examples, such as McIver is useful here. (For details see publications in the resources section.) More advanced grammar can be introduced gradually as suitable, for example,

grammar text

the colon and the semicolon. I always think this makes the work stand out if they are used for lists etc.

I also introduce the use of a dictionary. Most pupils use dictionaries at school but not habitually. They also use basic primary school dictionaries. I always use a large single volume dictionary such as "Collins Concise" as much of the requisite vocabulary is not contained in the primary school dictionaries. Good dictionaries to use are:

Collins Concise

Chambers

Macmillan

Large Oxford (single, one volume)

(To my mind the best dictionary to use is the two volume Shorter Oxford, which is an excellent work of reference for the family library, but too cumbersome for a 10 year old pupil.).

There may be some resistance to looking up words in a huge 1000 page text, but practice tends to overcome this issue. In addition, many pupils nowadays use on-line dictionaries to define words. I am not a fan of this, partly because I am old-fashioned and also because I like to look at the etymology and the surrounding words. I always encourage parents to purchase/use a good quality dictionary, for example, how many parents know that the term "algebra "is of Arabic origin and literally means "bone setting or reunion of broken parts" harking back to the Muslim scholars in North Africa during the Dark Ages?

In summary:

- Lessons should be for a minimum of one hour per week
- Tutoring should ideally begin 12-15 months prior to the examination
- Write answers to comprehension passages in full
- Give lots of praise and encouragement
- During Year 5 progress to past papers

- Use a suitable dictionary.

PROSPECTIVE PLANNING TIMETABLE – YEARS 4 -5

1. Year 4 – during the summer term weekly lessons or lessons on alternate weeks can commence. This is to give an introduction to working at home.

2. Year 5 – one lesson per week with a homework set every week in English. Pupils should be beginning to work an extra hour per week on another topic e.g. maths, verbal and non-verbal reasoning. After Christmas in Year 5, pupils will need to do one formal lesson per week plus two hours independently (subject to their skills).

3. After Easter in Year 5, pupils should be doing three hours per week of maths, English, verbal reasoning and non-verbal reasoning and focussing on completing the papers within the time frame necessary. Speed and accuracy go together and both are vital.

4. Many pupils and parents see it as important to work over the summer holidays to maintain the rhythm of working patterns set in the summer term of Year 5. I often work with pupils throughout the summer holidays, sometimes two lessons per week (or more) as September approaches.

5. Some 11+ examinations are set in September and some in January, so candidates should have honed their skills in order to be ready by August of that year (or the preceding year for January exams). Of course, pupils take family holidays and they need breaks during the summer too. The programme set out may seem quite intensive but in my experience, working to this general timetable leads to a high percentage of successful applications. Some people may disagree and think this is too much. On the other hand, some parents work their children much harder than this, putting in two or three hours at the

weekend and also after school. One size does not fit all, but steady and safe technical progress is bound to improve pupils' skills and knowledge.

6. Encourage the habits of writing, and also reading and sitting practice test papers.

HOMEWORK

Every week from when tuition begins, I set a written homework. I define this in terms of word length beginning at about 120 words per homework and building up to 300 words per homework (approximately). This is to encourage writing and writing skills over time. Most pupils will soon be able to extend their work more than they would have imagined. The word count is important because pupils may be resistant to writing at all and try to get away with as little as possible. Or at the opposite end, pupils tend to ramble for pages, generally producing very tedious prose. Paragraphing needs to be introduced from an early stage so that it becomes habitual. Pupils' vocabulary can be extended by requesting or giving lists of adjectives to insert into the prose, and generally grammar can be marked every week and improved. The *content* of the essays is really secondary to the *form* of good quality writing. There are lots of easy subjects, which fall into two main categories – fiction and non-fiction. For example, a short list for non-fiction could be as follows:

My amazing holiday

My best day out

My incredible journey

My favourite sport

Write 200 words on football

How to look after a pet.

My favourite pet.

The list can go on and on. It should include anything that sparks and holds the child's interest and which will therefore help them to write better prose. I often ask pupils to find out about writers that we have been studying e.g. "Write me 300 words about William Blake". Parents often help and use the internet to get raw data which can be processed. Gradually, the pupil becomes more independent and confident in their ability to write a structured passage of 300 words. This is the target length because schools request a written passage in the examination, the timescale usually being 30 or so minutes and

300 words corresponds to a full side of A4 paper for most pupils.

There are a myriad of techniques to assist in story writing and essay writing. A system of four or five story boards can be useful. These are pictures that tell a story. If the pupil has difficulty "starting the story", then when homework is set introductory sentences can be agreed together for each prospective paragraph. This means that the work will be partly laid out in advance. Parents often contribute their ideas and prose phrasing as well as encouragement and I often ask pupils "How much of this is your mother's writing?" This is not a criticism, as all of this input is helping the pupil to learn and progress to improve their skills.

Pupils should build up to a length of 300 words during Year 5 to give them confidence in the examination and produce a reservoir of writing behind them to draw on. Pupils can find imaginative writing very difficult or pupils can be too imaginative and continually introduce phenomena such as "aliens" or "spaceships" inappropriately into their narrative. A balance has to be found to encourage creative writing, which is 'fantasy' only when required. The point of this repetition is to be able to improve the quality of the prose, which is central to any story. I often encourage pupils to go through the five senses:

Touch

Vision

Sound

Taste

Smell

and encourage them to write a sentence for each when introducing a sense of place into a narrative. This, in some ways, may be the most difficult of tasks for those pupils who do not have a gift for writing. The writing has to be a bit 'special' to do well. Pupils must be trained to continue the story and/or write about what happened next, often a question for 11+ exam papers. Often, the key to success in this is to follow the "register" or style of the original passage and not engage in wild, fictitious episodes, but to maintain the emotional status of the given text and continue the narrative in a relevant way. This is easier said than done in most instances.

How to model for writing

a) What do we need to know? (context). Two or three ideas on place, time and characters.
b) Place this context in a model of three to five paragraphs.
c) Try to encourage individual ideas. Discuss these ideas and encourage parents to help. This encourages regular writing.
d) Each week, alternate between creative writing and non-fiction 'reporting', or narrative.
e) Confidence will gradually grow and input from other people, such as parents and siblings, often helps to give ideas as to the content of the prose before it is seen and corrected.

In summary:

- Set written homework at the end of every lesson
- Use storyboards if necessary

- Build up to a length of approximately 300 words during Year 5

PACE AND TIMING IN YEAR 5

By the time the pupil gets to Year 5 they have become used to a regular lesson and to working to 'order'. They are more relaxed and often even look forward to being tutored!

***

After an appropriate time tutoring from comprehension books, (this may be a few weeks or a few months), I move on to past papers from public schools, both 10+ and 11+. I have a library of such papers, many of which may be obtained on line. For example, Haberdashers Aske, City of London, Manchester Grammar School, Westminster, Dulwich, The Pearse School, etc. This is not a London-based focus but the more difficult papers tend to be from the top London schools. I discriminate, to begin with, by giving or setting what I regard to be simpler, more accessible papers to pupils. When I begin this paper based comprehension approach, I place no focus on time at the beginning, as we are practising to gain knowledge and experience. After a few months of working on papers exclusively, I encourage pupils to be aware of examination time and how long it takes to write responses to all the questions. This, of course, is going to vary tremendously between pupils, but as we move into Year 5, I look at marking as well and make it clear that to be successful we will need to attain a target mark of 85% in English.

It is also very important to agree with parents that to stand a good chance of getting in to the school of choice, they must encourage or facilitate the pupil to work on papers independently of my tuition sessions. Given that the pupil will have to become proficient in English, Maths, Verbal and Non-Verbal Reasoning papers, then often an hour a day after school is necessary to gain fluency, expertise and the experience needed to do well. Some parents encourage two hours a day towards the end of Year 5 and through the summer holidays prior to sitting the examination. This may sound hard and uncaring, and I do not necessarily recommend it, but I note that parents who set up a system such as this are almost invariably successful in attaining their school of choice. As I mentioned earlier, I only usually do one lesson a week with pupils, but I do strongly recommend that a lot more work has to be undertaken on a weekly basis to ensure success. Given the right spirit of endeavour in the home, most children will rise to the occasion and do well and work hard. This practice of working very hard can overcome some inabilities that the child may have. Not all pupils are gifted academically or find that good English skills come easily. However, technique and hard work can do surprising things to their standard of literacy and writing.

Year 5 (the earlier part) is a good time to work through Angus Maciver "First Aid in English" as a set series of homework to expand skills, knowledge and vocabulary. Not all pupils will need to do this as the more able pupils may have a more gifted sensibility in the use of language.

Multiple Choice Questions

These are becoming more popular as a means of testing so it is important to say something about them and the issues and problems that may be involved. There are some multiple choice worked examples to be found in the comprehension section.

Timing is also important in multiple choice questions and verbal reasoning. These may be approached through a series such as the Bond books which are age-graded. It is not necessary to do whole papers at once; pupils may address ten questions or so within a defined time period, for example, one minute per question and gradually work up speed as familiarity encourages progress and confidence. Some of the multiple choice questions (which seem to be increasingly used in comprehension passages as well) are very tricky. Two or three answers may be very similar and rely on subtle nuances of meaning. Pupils must be trained not to spend too much time trying to get the answers right on the one or two difficult questions which may appear. This may be very difficult as pupils always want to do well but there is a danger of using huge amounts of time on one question. Technique must be to spend a minute or so and then resolve to return to the question at the end of the paper if time allows. Some of these questions are tricky for adults and may require fine shades of meaning. Guessing is not to be encouraged but if the pupil is running out of time it is better to give an answer and responses may be honed. If there are five options, and two are obviously wrong, one may be possible and two probable, there is a place for responding with intelligence if the pupil is not 100% sure of the answer.

Timing, Timing, Timing!

I cannot stress enough that timing becomes more important as Year 5 progresses. It is surprising though, how the pupil can speed up tremendously when pushed a little and placed "on the clock" for even 10 minutes to do, for example, 10 verbal reasoning questions and consequently, find a great sense of achievement in being able to do all 10 questions in 9 – 10 minutes! Good timing practice gives a lot of confidence in showing what they are capable of.

Not answering questions in an examination due to lack of time is a major problem, so towards the end of the summer term, I recommend pupils practise working on lots of timed papers, but only when their confidence and skills are good. Everyone will progress at their own pace, but it can be very surprising to see how pupils pick up speed and accuracy, and when placed under a moderate amount of pressure, they can be very pleased with their progress. Competition is intense and unfortunately, speed and accuracy at this stage are vital. In addition, I always encourage the introduction of more interesting vocabulary as a matter of course to attract a good response from the examiner. I encourage pupils to work to a standard of 85% in English papers. This is hard, and may be impossible, but this is the target that seems to work with parents and pupils. It is a gauge of confidence in success. A bright, well-trained pupil can get to this level, but for some it will not be easy at all.

In summary:

- In Year 5 move onto past papers
- Increase the amount of time spent generally
- Work on multiple choice questions
- Learn to use a good dictionary
- Practice timing

PART II

"When I use a word," Humpty Dumpty said in a rather scornful tone, "it means what I choose it to mean - neither more nor less"

VOCABULARY IS VITAL!

This section discusses what language and vocabulary is necessary to sit the 11+, how important vocabulary is, and how to introduce more vocabulary into everyday writing.

***

Vocabulary is one of the most significant and important areas for the 11+. This is because those pupils with good, outstanding, or even just different vocabulary will attract the examiner's attention and gain marks. A very large part of the 11+ examination in English is to do with vocabulary; its acquisition and utilisation. Pupils weak in vocabulary will not be able to understand the comprehension passage (or passages) and therefore will not be able to answer the questions properly. This is a central point and cannot be stressed enough. From this point of vocabulary flows a lot of the methods and practice needed to successfully pass the 11+. How is vocabulary attained?

- Through ordinary everyday speech
- through primary schooling
- through reading.

Everyday language and primary school teaching, even if taken together, do not provide enough vocabulary to approach the 11+ with confidence.

Reading and the Classics

This leads us on to one of the main points of preparation, which is, of course, reading. Reading today for primary school age children is very piecemeal. The vocabulary learned in primary school is, of course, good and appropriate for most purposes and pupils, but the benchmark is much higher when approaching this examination. Television and the internet seem to have taken over the perception of language for the generation under the age of 11. Reading is good in any form because it extends literary skills, vocabulary and engenders a knowledge of grammar in the subconscious. Although books such as the Harry Potter series have been praised for extending the reading skills of pupils aged 8, 9 and 10, and similarly, an earlier generation was enthralled by Roald Dahl, I rarely recommend contemporary works of this nature, not because they are of poor quality or because of the entertaining and engaging nature of the stories, but merely because of their proscribed and sometimes limited vocabulary. (I would mention that Roald Dahl has been used in 10+ papers and

JK Rowling in 8+ papers). Why is this? It is because many of the elite 11+ schools use the "classics" almost exclusively in their comprehension tests so, by definition, pupils need to read the classics, both for the vocabulary, language structure and the narrative and also to learn about the characters, in order that they are familiar with these classic works.

You will find authors such as Dickens, Jules Verne, J M Barrie, Lewis Carroll, CS Lewis all vying for attention, using language that is not only unfamiliar but vocabulary which is entirely impenetrable to the 10 year old mind. This is not because modern children are stupid, but because they have never been exposed to this sort of language before. Please note anecdotally, that Dickens' "A Christmas Carol" is frequently used as a comprehension piece with obscure words such as "misanthropic" a word with which many parents would have some trouble. For example:

> "The water- plug being left in solitude, its overflowing sullenly congealed, and turned to misanthropic ice".

What vocabulary! "sullenly", "congealed" and "misanthropic" all in the same sentence.

I have heard it said that examiners include difficult language in some comprehension papers knowing full well that the children will have never encountered this language before and in fact, they are looking for pupils to guess the meaning, but I don't know if this is entirely true or just subjective conjecture.

Following on from this idea is the urgent need to extend, explore and be familiar with a vocabulary which is not generally given in schools and which is not in modern usage and will not be uncovered or encountered in day to day speech patterns. Therefore, I recommend repeatedly the need to read the classics. Many pupils are resistant to this and so parents are recommended to read them together with the child. Once begun, 95% of intelligent, aware children are enthralled by these texts, even if they find reading a chore. Reading the classics can be a great barrier to the progress of pupils in an electronic culture but parents must prevail and try to uncover ways, even in small doses, of exposing children to these great works. Personally, I love Roald Dahl and some other modern writers, but I do not generally recommend them as my focus is to get pupils through the examination. I always provide a short list of classics, (see Part 3) which most parents know of and I stress over and over again the importance of reading them in order to be exposed to their narrative and their language.

A technique for progress can be reading a chapter (or chapters) of a classic text for homework. This all depends on the child and their ability, skills and development and also their age. The technique is to set a written homework describing or summarising a particular chapter of the work (e.g. "The Hobbit" which is very popular with 10 year olds) each week or every other week until the text is completed. Some pupils cannot manage this and it needs to be seen as a long-term effort. Short homework can also be set on words that have not been covered and are not fully understood. Pupils can write a sentence to define half a dozen or so new words encountered so that they are thoroughly understood. Flash cards can be useful here and can be purchased on line. In addition, lists of words can be found in many books of grammar or on the internet.

Common errors:

- "which" and "witch";
- "now" and "know"
- "threw" and "through"
- "their" and "there"

Separate 'short' sessions can be given to test the pupil using flash cards, many of which have definitions of the word displayed. They are useful in that lots of new words can be found and used when writing essays. This is a great way to expand word knowledge and make writing more detailed and interesting.

Much of the mystique of the 11+ can be explained by application to the classics and by an almost 19th century approach to language and culture which residually remains in the examination process. Pupils are being exposed to a world of literature which has partly passed from view in the electronic culture that we now inhabit. This is one reason, but not the only reason, why even very good primary schools have no great value in preparing pupils for the elite schools and the 11+ in general. I frequently tell parents that even though primary school education is very good and useful to children, this will not necessarily provide the skills needed to pass the 11+. This is not to say that the schools are bad in general; they do provide a wealth of topics for pupils but we need to be very clear that they do not and cannot prepare them for the 11+ exam, as this is not their role. Bright pupils are generally not pushed enough in the state system. This is something I have experienced every week over years of tuition and teaching.

So to recap, a keystone is vocabulary. This is further explored in the section on teaching and writing.

In summary:

- Vocabulary is key
- Reading leads to improved vocabulary
- Concentrate on studying the classics
- List new words/use flash cards

CREATIVE WRITING

Almost every English examination has an approximately 30 - 40 minute comprehension test followed by a 30 minute section for descriptive or 'creative' writing.

For creative writing, I focus on the provision of three literary devices which are: metaphor, alliteration and simile. For the year up to the examination I require that every creative piece contains these devices, so that it becomes second nature to place them in any narrative. The inclusion of these devices will greatly enhance marks, irrespective of the general lyrical quality of the prose. It takes some time to do this, but with patience it can be achieved. Give examples and illustrations of metaphors. Illustration encourages the writer.

Following from the above, a general guide that I recommend to parents for writing vocabulary and grammar is the well-trusted "The New First Aid in English" by Angus Maciver published by Hodder Education and available to buy or order from any good bookshop or an online retailer. This book is a paragon for pedagogues like me and parents have told me that working through this text would be all that is needed for their child to sail through the 11+. It has a list of similes and many lists of words as well as comprehension passages. It is wonderfully old-fashioned which is why it is so suitable for the 11+. For example, in relation to vocabulary it works with much language that is no longer used but which may be found in 11+ comprehension papers. How many pupils today would know that 'a score' means 20 or that 'a baker's dozen' means 13? The book is also full of proverbs and phrases which have slipped out of the language. It was first published in 1938 and has been updated many times, is cheap, invaluable and comes with its own separate answer book, which is of great value for parent, tutor and teacher alike.

At the start of every lesson, last week's written homework should be examined, marked, commented on and praised copiously. Spellings may be extracted for further testing and creative criticism written at the bottom. New literary devices may be commented on; "you could have put it like this" or "what about including these adjectives" etc. The grammar may be corrected and extended in a way that encourages more sophisticated devices. Pupils seem to learn very quickly like this, they are always anxious to please, and the intensity of a one-to-one tuition setting can be very productive in making great advances in writing skills, styles, genres etc. All of this occurs organically without obsession or pretension or excessive pressure on the pupil. It is a natural process and learning takes place at the correct pace for each individual. Always praise a lot, use a dictionary and if the pupil is obviously struggling with the issue of endurance, performing the same technique of writing comprehension, then I break off and do a dictation, or spelling or short grammar exercise.

It is important that the pupil is aware of the need to be legible and if bad handwriting is a problem, then the pupil should practice this as a priority, as marks can be lost if the script is unintelligible.

In summary:

- Learn the meanings of metaphor, alliteration and simile. Also personification could be included.
- Extend the pupil's knowledge by using suitable reference books
- Mark homework at the beginning of the lesson
- Ensure the pupil is aware of the need for legibility

DICTATION

A dictation passage is usually taken from a classic text, such as Tolkien. I offer the pupil a short passage of a classic and suggest that they choose two or three sentences or a short paragraph for dictation. This will take about 10 minutes. The pupil should read through the passage looking, in particular, for grammar and spelling. I then dictate until the passage is completed and I read through again to place emphasis on the grammatical structure and ask the pupil to listen carefully to my voice and to punctuate accordingly.

This practice has fallen out of favour in schools for some reason. I think this is very useful as it constrains the pupil to think very carefully about punctuation, capital letters and even brackets and hyphens. Much of this grammar is rarely found in primary readers. Writers like Dickens often have long convoluted sentences containing intricate metaphors which need to be deconstructed. The whole exercise has much value in addition to spelling and vocabulary. I always suggest that pupils guess the number of mistakes that they have made before we mark it and I always stress that making mistakes is good for learning. Pupils seem to enjoy this exercise perhaps because it gives them independence and they do not do it in school. It can be seen as competing with yourself. In any event, I find giving dictation diverting and valuable educationally.

In summary:

- Dictation is useful for spelling
- Dictation is very useful for learning grammar and syntax
- Dictation gives the pupil confidence in writing.

'Reeling and Writhing, of course, to begin with,' the Mock Turtle replied: 'and then the different branches of Arithmetic - Ambition, Distraction, Uglification, and Derision'.

OTHER TOPICS

Mathematics

In mathematics, it is useful to work towards 90% correct answers. The City of London School is most useful in this respect (as is Latymer School), as they provide answers to their past papers (if you can get hold of them). There is a big issue with mathematics which is the fact that some topics which are in the examination will not have been studied by pupils by the end of Year 5 but will be studied in Year 6 after the examination, so work in mathematics will often be a process of discovering areas in which the child lacks knowledge, for example, indices or basic algebra and then covering these topics to bring the pupil up to speed. In addition to this, there may be issues with the curriculum. Pupils today study topics which their parents did not study, such as symmetry and probability, of which the parents may have no knowledge. Also maths is taught differently every five or ten years in relation to how long division or long multiplication are laid out so the parent may not be *au fait* or up to speed with contemporary techniques of mathematical calculation. I always tell the pupil that it doesn't matter how you get to the right answer as long as they do get the right answer. I tend to show pupils my methods learned in the 1950s but I am not dogmatic about this. Although some people strongly disagree with this idea, young minds are flexible and eager to attain new skills and do not possess some of the prejudices of their elders. Most pupils I teach tend to be better at maths than I am!

Lots of children need to practise their mental arithmetical skills for quick simple calculations in order to speed up their mental processes. They have to have quick mental maths skills to hand and practice can make pupils much quicker in this area. Accurate and fast command of the times table is absolutely essential.

Two other problems with maths are language and sequencing. Firstly, language. Pupils often don't understand questions that are framed differently from the language they are used to. For example: "what is the product of 10 x 14?" Many pupils will never have heard the word "product" or "function" in this context and this can completely "throw" them even though they actually know the answer when couched in terms they understand. This can be a big problem so careful study of past papers is essential as forms of layout and language can vary widely.

The second issue is 'sequencing'. Some complex questions require two or three separate calculations, one following on from the other, and pupils are not trained in this area. They need to be taught to look for and understand how the question is laid out or formatted.

These issues can easily be overcome, but it is why practice is so important. In general, work to the level of 85% to 90% on the papers and make sure that errors are fully investigated and resolved.

The reasons why answers can be wrong generally fall into three groups:

1. Reading the question incorrectly or too quickly. (We all do this!) Practice reading and re-reading several times if necessary.

2. Errors of calculation, often quite simple, due to lack of attention or a careless approach. This is also an area where accurate knowledge of the times tables is crucial.

3. Lack of knowledge on how to answer the question, for example: "I don't know what the internal angles of a triangle are so I can't do the question!"

In summary:

- Work to 90% correct as a target
- Do lots of past papers
- Fill in 'gaps' in knowledge
- Carefully go through the answers that are wrong to analyse the technique or reasons why

VERBAL AND NON-VERBAL REASONING

As you might expect, "vocabulary, vocabulary, vocabulary" is the mantra for verbal reasoning. A poor vocabulary will mean a lot of questions will be answered incorrectly. Sometimes simple words are not readily understood by 10 year olds and these are often skimmed over. Also, many of the questions combine English and mathematics in "sequencing" that is, maths-style questions are written out in full language. There are also alphabetical codes, which rely on mastery of the alphabet. Practice is the only method of discovering areas of weakness and when techniques become more familiar, and then speed and accuracy will follow. As with non-verbal reasoning, flexible young minds adjust rapidly and with interest to take command of the areas undertaken.

In my experience, 10 and 11 year olds are better at non-verbal reasoning than adults. These tests remind me of the classic "intelligence tests" (IQ) by Hans Eysenck published in the 1960s. They have to do with spatial awareness, sequencing and order. They are infuriating tests in my opinion but they still must be approached with the right degree of diligence.

Again, start off slowly with a practice booklet, maybe only 10 questions at a time, until over a period of weeks, the pupil becomes familiar with and trained in the methods and techniques required. There are many sets of test papers available but they must have answers to be of practical use. You must always work through the questions the pupil has got wrong, working back from the answer to gain an understanding of where the pupil went wrong. Speed should be built up over time as well. Always impress on the pupil the importance of not spending too long on a difficult question. It is best to go through the exam paper, answer all the questions which can be done immediately, and then go through the paper again and try to answer the questions that have been missed out because they are difficult and require more effort. This ensures that the pupil gains all the marks they can. This may be obvious, but it is sometimes overlooked as an exam strategy and is vital. Exam technique can raise marks in an exam dramatically and is very important. 30% of what I teach is technique as well knowledge and vocabulary. It is no good getting half the questions right and running out of time for the other half.

In summary:

- Vocabulary (again!)
- Technical planning on how to answer questions is vital
- Carefully go over questions that were wrong
- Exam timing

"It's a poor sort of memory that only works backwards" says the White Queen to Alice.

IN GENERAL

Pupil Stress

Stress may be an issue for your child. All children are different but most will respond well to a clearly set out programme of work, which has parental control and support. Very often I have seen parents become extremely anxious in relation to progress, especially if it does not meet their expectations and this can be a serious issue, as parental anxiety is often picked up by the child, either consciously or subconsciously. It would help, in my opinion, if parents made it clear to their children that failure in the 11+ examination is not the end of the world. There are other opportunities to take examinations for top schools e.g. 13+ or even at A level if necessary. It is worth noting that grammar schools (following the Greek model) were only ever designed for 10% of the population and grammar schools (and high academic achievement generally) are not suited to everyone and may indeed be inappropriate.

If you think your child is suffering from stress, it may be best to give them a break, for example, a day at the beach or walking in the countryside or a trip to a theme park can be of great benefit and will help them start again with renewed enthusiasm and, of course, time off should be built into their weekly timetable.

Marking

Marking should always be done immediately at the beginning of the next lesson. This gives a sense of continuity and keeps it up to date with a recent memory of the work done. 11+ pupils often talk to me about their homework as soon as I get to the house, before I have even sat down. There is an enthusiasm and immediacy for the work that they have just completed. Pupils actively seek approval and praise and verification of the work that they have done. I always mark in green or purple pen, never red, as red always hints at anger. At the beginning of tuition, I do not correct all of the errors if there are a lot, as this may be discouraging, but after a few weeks or months, I am more exacting in my corrections. I write out misspelt words at the bottom of the text and they write out sentences that need to be reconstructed. I may also go through any grammar that needs attention. I always write positive comments of some description at the bottom for encouragement, such as "well done", "good work", ("needs to be longer") ("please use paragraphs"). The main point is not to be parsimonious with praise. However, one must remember the point of writing is to encourage better skills and repetition of writing facility. I sometimes put adjectives or conjunctives at the bottom that might be entered into the prose as an alternative. Many pupils are very good at marking their own work when I point out an error to them. If we go over the prose, they naturally correct it themselves when prompted. This just confirms a lack of concentration or focus and I reassure them that they knew the correct answer anyway.

The Importance of Setting for tuition

This can be quite important. A desk or kitchen table without distractions is ideal. On occasion, I have had parents sitting in the same room whilst I am teaching which I find quite unnerving and not really conducive to a teaching/learning situation. I find it best to sit side by side with the pupil rather than at opposite sides of the table as I am often pointing to the prose with a pen to indicate words, paragraphs, passages etc and also to clearly see the pupil's written responses to questions. I usually teach in the evenings and I prefer to have a parent or another adult somewhere in the property in an adjacent room. Lighting might be important. All these trivial asides combine to assist in creating the right atmosphere. 90% of the time I am given tea and sometimes, I am offered more food than I can eat and I sometimes have difficulty eating and talking! After the first lesson, parents are usually happy to leave me on my own in a room with the child. In my experience, most families (from all cultures) are very hospitable, grateful and welcoming.

Sitting the Exam

Make sure your child has adequate sleep the night before and is equipped with all the necessary stationery, spare pens etc so that the day itself goes smoothly on a practical level. It is most important to avoid any anxiety building up if at all possible, so plan ahead, keep calm yourself and allow plenty of time to ensure that the pupil arrives early at the examination venue.

PART III

EXAMPLE COMPREHENSION EXERCISES

N.B. These three passages are not a workbook but demonstrate teaching methods when it comes to tackling comprehension exercises for all ages.

First Passage

From "The Railway Children" by E Nesbit.

The three children, Bobby the oldest, Peter the second oldest, and Phyllis the youngest, encounter a life-threatening landslide whilst out hunting for cherries. The landslide blocks the main railway line.

"It's *all* coming down" Peter tried to say, but he found there was hardly any voice to say it with. And, indeed, just as he spoke, the great rock, on the top of which the walking trees were, leaned slowly forward. The trees, ceasing to walk, stood still and shivered. Leaning with the rock, they seemed to hesitate for a moment, and then rock and trees and grass and bushes, with a rushing sound, slipped right away from the face of the cutting and fell on the line with a blundering crash that could have been heard half a mile off. A cloud of dust rose up.

"Oh" said Peter in awestruck tones, "isn't it exactly like when coals come in? – if there wasn't any roof to the cellar and you could see down."

"Look what a great mound it's made!" said Bobbie.

"Yes, it's right across the down line," said Phyllis.

"That'll take some sweeping up" said Bobbie.

"Yes," said Peter, slowly. He was still leaning on the fence. "Yes" he said again, still more slowly.

Then he stood upright.

"The 11.29 down hasn't gone by yet. We must let them know at the station or there'll be a most frightful accident".

"Let's run, said Bobbie, and began.

But Peter cried, "Come back!" and looked at Mother's watch. He was very prompt and businesslike, and his face looked whiter than they had ever seen it.

"No time" he said; "it's two miles away, and it's past eleven".

"Couldn't we" suggested Phyllis, breathlessly, "couldn't we climb on a telegraph post and do something to the wires?"

"We don't know" said Peter.

"They do it in war" said Phyllis; "I know I've heard of it".

"They only *cut* them silly," said Peter, "and that doesn't do any good. And we couldn't cut them even if we got up, and we couldn't get up. If we had anything red, we could get down the line and wave it".

"But the train wouldn't see us till it got round the corner, and then it could see the mound as well as us" said Phyllis; "better, because it's much bigger than us".

"If we only had something red" Peter repeated, "we could go round the corner and wave to the train".

"We might wave anyway".

"They'd only think it was just *us,* as usual. We've waved so often before. Anyway, let's get down."

They got down the steep stairs. Bobbie was pale and shivering. Peter's face looked thinner than usual. Phyllis was red-faced and damp with anxiety.

"Oh, how hot I am!" she said; "and I thought it was going to be cold; I wish we hadn't put on our –" she stopped short, and then ended in a different tone – "our flannel petticoats".

Bobbie turned at the bottom of the stairs.

"Oh yes" she cried; "*they're* red! Let's take them off".

They did, and with the petticoats rolled up under their arms, ran along the railway, skirting the newly fallen mound of stones and rock and earth, and bent, crushed, twisted trees. They ran at their best pace. Peter led, but the girls were not far behind. They reached the corner that hid the mound from the straight line of the railway that ran half a mile without a curve or corner.

"Now" said Peter, taking hold of the largest flannel petticoat.

"You're not" – Phyllis faltered – "you're not going to *tear* them?"

"Shut up" said Peter with brief sternness.

"Oh yes" said Bobbie "tear them into little bits if you like. Don't you see, Phil, if we can't stop the train, there'll be a real live accident with people *killed*. Oh, horrible!..."

Questions

1. Give two short phrases which illustrate the two different characters and explain the differences in these phrases of:

   (a) Peter
   (b) Phyllis.

(six marks).

2. How do we know that this book was written over a 100 years ago? Give examples of any clues which illustrate this. (three marks)

3. Explain how the writer makes the first paragraph interesting and engaging to the reader. Please use details from the passage. (eight marks)

4. In the first quarter of the passage, how does the author show us that Peter is thinking carefully about the situation? (four marks).

5. Find a word in the passage which means the same as
   (a) To go around;
   (b) Nervousness;
   (c) Barging into.
   (d) Hesitated.

(four marks)

Answers

1. Various examples from the text. For example, "he was very prompt and businesslike"; "'shut up' said Peter

with brief sternness". This is Peter pretending to be an adult and wanting to be a leader. Secondly for Phyllis when she says "' you're not going to tear them' "; and " ' Oh, how hot I am!' ". These phrases show her spontaneity and the fact that when she thinks she speaks.

2.   There are several references in the text. The list could include:

Flannel petticoats

Coals coming into the cellar

Telegraph post

(Pupils may also refer to the lack of any modern communication systems such as a mobile phone)

This question is quite difficult and requires close reading of the text and an intuitive mind.

3.   "The trees ceasing to walk stood still and shivered" or "the walking trees" or "trees leaning with the rock seemed to

hesitate a moment". What is needed here are details from the passage and also to explain and quote the idea of personification. The pupil may not know what personification is so I would ask the child if they know what a metaphor is. Children have usually touched upon metaphor at Key Stage 2 but they are not particularly strong in this area. Therefore, I would break off from the text and talk about what a metaphor is.

This again leads us back to whether the child understands a simile as literary device. We go backwards in order to prepare the ground for going forwards. This is very necessary and is part of the learning process. Pupils are often embarrassed to clearly state that they do not know what a metaphor or a simile is so I would give them exercises to do e.g. three to five examples. Firstly, to write what is simile is and a list e.g.

> 'The light was as bright as the sun'.

'It was sharp as a knife'.

'It was black as the night'.

We need to have a good basis of understanding here so we may pause then to look at metaphors and compare the two. e.g. 'my brother eats like a pig'; 'my brother is a pig at the dining table'. I give a few oral examples and then a few written examples from memory or from a handy text and then ensure that part of any homework includes a short exercise on similes, metaphors, and personification, as appropriate.

Generally speaking, personification is a bit more difficult to use as a matter of habit or to interpret from a passage. Oscar Wilde is particularly good at this in his stories for children, for example, "The Giant's Garden".

Angus Maciver gives a copious list of similes, particularly pertaining to the qualities of things e.g. "as cold as charity" "as flat as a flounder" (a fish) and he gives many entertaining, old-fashioned similes.

Exercises may be set at this point. It is important to encourage the writing of proper short quotations here, to create a habit with the pupil. Again, pupils may not know what a quotation is and how to write one down with speech marks/quotation marks and the proper grammatical context, so time may be fruitfully spent doing this. I often write down a couple of quotes to explain and give an example. The whole point is that you are training and educating in grammar from a worked example. What quotations might we give? An example of personification would be the sentence "the trees, ceasing to walk, stood still and shivered". Further to this, we might mention the language "a rushing sound" and/or "a blundering crash" as examples of interesting and vivid language. We might also note that the passage moves from a sense of visual movement to sound. We would not expect pupils to pick up all of these points, but the bright pupil will learn and 'take on board' these techniques and over time, we will refine them together to produce work of a consistently high standard.

4. To answer this question properly is quite difficult. It would require the pupil to find the exact point and either explain it and/or quote it in full or in part. For example, we know that the author explains Peter's thought processes; he says "yes" slowly and "'Yes' he said again still more slowly". The next line confirms that he has finished thinking by stating "then he stood upright". Any part of this analysis would gain two marks as long as it communicates an understanding. I repeat, this is a difficult question and requires focus and maturity of analysis.

5. (a) skirting

(b) anxiety

(c) blundering

(d) faltered

Second Passage

From "A Christmas Carol" by Charles Dickens

At length the hour of shutting up the counting-house arrived. With an ill-will Scrooge dismounted from his stool, and tacitly admitted the fact to the expectant clerk in the Tank, who instantly snuffed his candle out, and put on his hat.

"You'll want all day tomorrow, I suppose?" said Scrooge.

"If quite convenient, sir".

"It's not convenient" said Scrooge, "and it's not fair. If I was to stop half-a-crown for it, you'd think yourself ill-used I'll be bound?"

The clerk smiled faintly.

"And yet," said Scrooge, "you don't think me ill-used, when I pay a day's wages for no work".

The clerk observed that it was only once year.

"A poor excuse for picking a man's pocket every twenty-fifth of December!" said Scrooge, buttoning his great-coat to the chin. "But I suppose you must have the whole day. Be here all the earlier next morning".

The clerk promised that he would and Scrooge walked out with a growl. The office was closed in a twinkling, and the clerk, with the long ends of his white comforter dangling below his waist (for he boasted no great-coat) went down a slide on Cornhill, at the end of a lane of boys, twenty times, in honour of its being Christmas Eve and then ran home to Camden Town as hard as he could pelt, to play at blindman's buff.

Scrooge took his melancholy dinner in his usual melancholy tavern, and having read all the newspapers, and beguiled the rest of the evening with his banker's-book, went home to bed. He lived in chambers which had once belonged to his deceased partner. They were a gloomy suite of rooms, in a lowering pile of building up a yard, where it had so little business to be, that one could scarcely help fancying it must have run there when it was a young house, playing at hide-and-seek with other houses, and forgotten the way out again. It was old enough now, and dreary enough, for nobody lived in it but Scrooge the other rooms all being let out as offices. The yard was so dark that even Scrooge, who knew its every stone, was fain to grope with his hands. The fog and frost so hung about the black old gateway of the house, that it seemed as if the Genius of the Weather sat in mournful meditation on the threshold.

Questions

1. The last paragraph gives two examples of personification. Describe one of these.

2. Explain in your own words from the last sentence i.e. "that it seemed as if the Genius of the Weather sat in mournful meditation on the threshold".

3. How does the author show in the first 14 lines of dialogue:

    (a) The character of the clerk?

    (b) Scrooge's character?

4. Give two examples in detail from the prose passage to show that it was written 150 years ago

5. Place "melancholy" in a sentence of your own construction.

6. What does "pelt" mean?

7. The clerk who works for Scrooge is called Bob Cratchit. Do you think you would like or dislike this character? Please give two details from the passage to support your view of him.

Answers

1.   Answer: "it must have run there when it was a young house..";

"it was old enough now".

The description should comment on the personification of the house that Dickens wrote about as if it was a human being and has the capacity to run about and get old.

2.   This is a tricky question because it is separated into two parts comprising comprehension and secondly, placing the response 'in your own words'. What often happens here is that pupils respond by only answering the comprehension passage and neglecting to put the prose into their own language. Pupils will need to find a synonym for "genius" (could mean "spirit"); mournful, (sad or gloomy); meditation, (thought/reflection); and "threshold"   (doorway/entrance). These are truly challenging words for a 10 year old to find synonyms for and the words themselves may not readily be understood. So it is a true test and more difficult than it appears.

3.   (a) He is polite e.g. "if quite convenient sir"; "smiled faintly". This shows he is subservient and has to do as instructed by   Scrooge.   "...with   ill   will

descended..." This shows he is generally bad tempered and mean.

(c) "it's not convenient.." This shows he is difficult and controlling.

4. References to "candle", "half a crown", "counting house", "great coat", "comforter" etc are good pointers.

5. Any well-written response.

6. To run fast.

7. Any intelligent responses, which include short quotations.

Multiple Choice Questions

8. In the last paragraph from which starts "Scrooge took his melancholy dinner" Scrooge is on his own all evening. Why is he alone?

Choose from the following:

(a) The tavern is empty so he has no one to be with.

(b) Scrooge does not have any friends that live nearby.

(c) He likes to be on his own; he is a solitary person.

(d) He is mean-spirited and cold-hearted so he has no friends.

9. Please choose the answer that is closest in meaning to the phrase "in a lowering pile of a building".

Choose from the following:

(a) The foundations of the buildings are sinking into the ground.

(b) You have to enter the building by going through a door in the basement.

(c) The building is grim and gloomy.

(d) The building is a construction site.

Answers to multiple choice questions:

8. The answer is (d). If we know the story Scrooge is on his own due to a failed relationship in his earlier life. If we only know the passage, we can see that he is very miserable and curmudgeonly. (c) would be a possible

answer but (d) gives a deeper reason for him being on his own.

9.   The answer is (c). This is dependent on the pupil on understanding the meaning of "lowering" which is a 19th century synonym for "depressing".

This passage is short but on a quick reading, we can find 14 words which are no longer in common usage or difficult for the average 10 year old and some of them would be difficult for the average adult too. These include:

Old word
Modern Meaning

Ill-used;
abused

Tank;
depressing small room

Half a crown;
old money

Comforter;
scarf

Blind Man's Buff;
children's game

Melancholy;
sad

Beguiled;
spent

Tacitly;
unspoken

Chambers;
rooms

Fancying;
imagining

Genius;
spirit

Fain;
obliged

Lowering
depressing

Pelt.
To run fast

In general, this passage from "A Christmas Carol" is difficult for almost everyone, even though it is very short. It is really quite important that the pupil should know the story of A Christmas Carol and have had some exposure to Dickens' language. Vocabulary is relatively impenetrable to the average reader; he uses such words as "tacit" and "beguiled" which most people would never have heard of. Everyone will get the general gist of the prose but the finer detail may escape them. There is a wonderful use of metaphor in Dickens, which livens his prose tremendously, but makes it hard for pupils to read it easily.

Dickens is often used as a prose passage for elite schools such as Haberdashers and City of London, so this reinforces the need for reading classical literature of this type. Pupils may need to be systematic in their reading and be scrupulously encouraged to use a good dictionary for some of these difficult words, a habit which is difficult to put into practice and why it is an advantage for them to read with an interested adult who can tease out and define challenging vocabulary. A curious pupil and an intelligent pupil will always ask about words they do not understand, but the average reader cannot be relied upon to do this. They will skip vocabulary and lose meaning and misinterpret words thus eventually leading to exam failure.

Third Passage

Introduction

Treasure Island is a classic story by Robert Louis Stevenson. In this passage we find that the main character, Jim Hawkins, is on Treasure Island; he is on his own trying to avoid the pirates when he sees a strange figure in the trees.

He was concealed by this time behind another tree trunk; but he must have been watching me closely, for as soon as I began to move in his direction he reappeared and took a step to meet me. Then he hesitated, drew back, came forward again, and at last, to my wonder and confusion, threw himself on his knees and held out his clasped hands in supplication.

At that I once more stopped.

'Who are you?' I asked.

'Ben Gunn,' he answered, and his voice sounded hoarse and awkward, like a rusty lock. 'I'm poor Ben Gunn, I am; and I haven't spoken with a Christian these three years.'

I could now see that he was a white man like myself, and that his features were even pleasing. His skin, wherever it was exposed, was burnt by the sun; even his lips were black; and his fair eyes looked quite startling in so dark a face. Of all the beggar-men that I had seen or fancied, he was the chief for raggedness. He was clothed with tatters of old ship's canvas and old seacloth; and this extraordinary patchwork was all held together by a system of the most various and incongruous fastenings, brass buttons, bits of stick, and loops of tarry gaskin. About his waist he wore an old brass-buckled leather belt which was the one thing solid in his whole accoutrement.

'Three years!' I cried, 'Were you shipwrecked?'

'Nay, mate,' said he- 'marooned'.

I had heard the word, and I knew it stood for a horrible kind of punishment common enough among the buccaneers, in which the offender is put ashore with a little powder and shot, and left behind on some desolate and distant island.

'Marooned three years agone,' he continued, 'and lived on goats since then and berries and oysters. Wherever a man is, says I, a man can do for himself. But mate, my heart is sore for Christian diet. You mightn't happen to have a piece of cheese about you now? No? Well, many's the long night I've dreamed of cheese- toasted mostly – and woke up again and here I were'.

'If ever I can get on board again,' said I ' you shall have cheese by the stone.'

All this time he had been feeling the stuff of my jacket, smoothing my hands, looking at my boots, and generally, in the intervals of his speech, showing a childish pleasure in the presence of a fellow-creature. But at my last words he perked up into a startled shyness.

Questions

1. Would you like Ben Gunn's character? Explain your reasons why. (one mark).

2. Describe in your own words what Ben Gunn looks like (six marks).

3. How do you think Ben Gunn feels after meeting another person for long? (six marks)

4. What two things has Ben Gunn missed most during his three years on the island? (four marks).

5. Write down one word from the passage which means the same as:

   (a) supplication (praying or begging)

   (b) tatters (rags)

   (c) incongruous (ill-fitting, out of place)

   (d) accoutrement (dress, outfit)

   (four marks)

6. Explain what the following words mean in the passage:

Marooned

Buccaneers

Powder and shot

Stone

(four marks for each answer)

6. Write a short paragraph of about three sentences to state the first things you would do if you were marooned on an island on your own.
(six marks)

Answers

1. Any intelligent and composed response which takes into account his attributes e.g. "raggedy" "eccentric" etc.

2. This is difficult as the pupil must give answers for words which are relatively obscure e.g:

   a. Tatters – rags, worn out clothes
   b. Canvas – sail
   c. Accoutrement – clothing
   d. "he looked like a scarecrow" etc
   e. Ragamuffin – archaic term for scruffy little boy

3. Answers which are sensitive to his emotional state – "shock", "overwhelmed" with detail on how he is unused to speaking English.

4. "Speech" and "cheese".

5. Given.

6. Marooned – to deliberately put a person on shore alone (by pirates)

   Buccaneers – another word for "pirate"

Powder and shot – ammunition for flint-lock muskets

"stone" – an imperial weight of approximately 6. Kg . (a lot of cheese!)

7. Any sensible response of three sentences which describes what would be need to be done e.g. finding food, clothing, shelter, preparing bonfire in terms of rescue. Any details such as this would attract full marks.

'And how many hours a day did you do lessons?' said Alice, in a hurry to change the subject.

'Ten hours the first day,' said the Mock Turtle: 'nine the next, and so on.'

'What a curious plan!' exclaimed Alice.

'That's the reason they're called lessons' the Gryphon remarked: 'because they lessen from day to day.'

EXAMPLE FORMAL LESSON PLAN

This is a practical guide to how I proceed during a lesson. There is no need to be fixed about this and much flexibility is necessarily built in, but for the newcomer, it may prove useful/valuable.

For the first five or ten minutes always go through the written homework for the last lesson in detail, writing comments at the bottom, spellings etc. You may also need to go through areas that need to be improved in the essay. These are, of course, related to the specific text, but generally it would be paragraphing, layout, syntax, vocabulary and general quality of the writing. I always make lots of positive comments even if it is of a low standard, as confidence is very important.

The main part of the lesson should be spent on a published comprehension passage or a past paper. This where pupils learn all the skills they need. Never just sit quietly and let the pupil work on their own; always interact, making suggestions and positive comments about how to approach the topic or questions. Explaining the questions is a vitally important facet of the work, as is reinforcing focus on the marking scheme. Timing of the writing may or may not be important, depending on where the pupil is in relation to the pending examination. I often have two or three papers and encourage the pupil to choose one which they think they would like to do based on author, content or length of the passage.

If I find that the pupil is "labouring" or not engaging after a period of time, then I introduce a different topic in the short term, possibly spellings that have accumulated from past essays that need to be tested, or break into mathematics for a time, to introduce variety. I try to always carry a maths paper in my bag for such occasions, as backup.

After this change of activity, I go back to the paper we were working on or try a different paper if this proves too difficult. Thus, the whole session is spent reading and writing. I often stress that it is a written exam. After 55 minutes I set homework, which is the standard format of 300 words on a topic, often given at the end of the exam paper. I make sure this is written down somewhere in a homework book or on a piece of paper given to the pupil and 70% of the time, I confirm this with the parent before I leave, pointing out where this is and what it is so that all three parties are clear as to what exactly needs to be done before the next lesson. This is quite a simple formula but it has stood the test of time and of course, can be modified to include specialist work as and when the need arises, for example, exercises on such grammatical or literary devices which need to be at the fingertips of every successful candidate, and also the meaning and use of similes and metaphors.

5 – 10 minutes:

Reading and analysis of last week's homework; doing corrections, spelling mistakes, alterations, positive and negative points; word count.

5 – 10 minutes:

Comprehension passage from past papers or work book as follows:

3 – 5 mins: reading the passage to be arrived at by negotiation; reading quietly, individually or alternately; questions to ask: "is this passage too difficult/too easy?" "do you understand the story?" Also highlight any obvious difficult vocabulary and even obscure metaphors if any.

35 minutes:

Answering the questions working as a team with the pupil at first setting the pace; if a pupil finds it difficult or gets bored for 35 minutes then break off to do other activities such as reading for 2-3 minutes, then returning to the text.

8 minutes (if time permits):

Short dictation – allow pupil to choose a passage of two to three sentences of a suitable passage for dictation; ask them how many mistakes they think they have made and mark it for punctuation, spelling etc. This can be extended if time and circumstances are appropriate but it is a good alternative activity to comprehension work.

last 2 minutes:

Set and read homework making sure it is understood and written down.

Make notes about the lesson e.g. difficulties with punctuation, spelling etc for your own reference.

LIST OF COMMONLY
MISSPELT WORDS

accelerate

accident

accommodation

argument

believe

business

calendar

category

changeable

chocolate

definite(ly)

embarrass

equipment

February

fiery

foreign

grateful

height

immediate

it's (short for "it is")

its (possessive)

now (present time)

know (have knowledge of)

knowledge

library

mischievous

neighbour

occasionally

physics

possession

practice (noun)

practise (verb)

recommend

rhyme

rhythm

separate

their (possessive plural)

there (place)

they're (short for "they are")

twelfth

until

weather/whether

Wednesday

This of course, is not a complete list of difficult misspelt words which can be found on the internet and there are also good spelling lists available in Angus Maciver's "First Aid in English". These are some of the most obvious and difficult words likely to be encountered by 10 year olds.

Try taking three to five words per week as a spelling test and encourage pupils to put them in their weekly writing assignment. If this is repeated, pupils will soon become comfortable with spelling these awful words. Lots of adults have difficulty with some of these words and a spell check is not available in a written examination.

THE USE OF THE APOSTROPHE

The apostrophe is like a pair of twins. They are identical but they both have their own personality and do things very differently.

Let us call them Twin A and Twin B.

Twin A always inserts itself into a sentence where it wants to show something **belongs** to something else. (This is known as the possessive.) For example, *the boy's ball* or *the baby's rattle.*

If there is more than one subject e.g. boys, not boy, the apostrophe always come AFTER the plural i.e. the boys' ball (more than one boy), the babies' rattle (more than one baby). If there is more than one ball it remains *the boys' balls* or *the babies' rattles.* The subject gets the apostrophe but not the object.

But what about group nouns?

A group noun such as 'children' is regarded as a single noun e.g. 'the children's playground'.

Twin B always inserts itself into a sentence where *it stands in for another letter or group of letters.* For example, *it's (it is) raining today* or *they're (they are) running for the bus.*

When you see a sentence which needs an apostrophe ask yourself the question:

Does this mean that something **belongs to** something else?

OR

Does this mean the apostrophe is **standing in for something which is missing (replacing a letter or group of letters)?**

Learning this rule will result in you always using the apostrophe in the correct way.

The Greengrocer's apostrophe.

So-called because greengrocers seem to have a propensity for inserting unnecessary apostrophes! Generally speaking, plurals never need an apostrophe (unless they are possessive as above). Many people think they do but this is invariably not the case, so be very sparing in your use of the apostrophe and do not sprinkle your work with unnecessary apostrophes, which will lose you marks (e.g. cabbages, leeks). There are some words that are irregular and a list is given in Angus Maciver's "First Aid in English" (page 215).

Exceptions to the Rule!

As ever with English grammar, there are extremely important exceptions to these rules, which **must** be learnt for good literacy:

Its and it's

The possessive "it" never has an apostrophe e.g. "The day had its usual spells of sunny weather" as opposed to: "It's very sunny for this time of year". In other words, *its* only has an apostrophe when it means *it is*.

IMPERIAL WEIGHTS AND MEASURES V METRIC

You may think this is an odd addition to this addendum but in fact, some non-verbal reasoning tests do test pupils on converting one to the other, so it is worthwhile learning the basic principles in case such a question is set during the exam:

Weights

One ounce (1 oz) = 28.35 gm

16 ounces = One pound (1 lb) – 453.59 gm.

1 stone = 14 lbs.= 6.35 kilo

112lbs = 1 hundredweight (cwt).

(just over 50 kilos)

20 cwt = 1 ton

(Therefore one pound is just under half a kilo)

Liquids

Two pints = 1 quart

8 pints -= 1 gallon

1 pint = 568.26 ml

1 quart = 1.14 litres

1 gallon = 4.55 litres

(therefore 1 pint is just over half a litre)

Measurements

1 inch (1") = 2.54 cm.

12" = 1 foot (1') = 30.48 cm

3 feet = 1 yard = 91.44 cm

1 mile = 1760 yards = 1.61 km

(therefore 1 yard is just under one metre)

(All Imperial figures stated refer to English standard measurements and not American which are not given).

A NOTE ON AVAILABLE RESOURCES

On-line English and Maths papers for 7+, 8+, 9+, 10+, 11+ and 13+ are available free. The majority of these papers are for 11+. For example:

City of London School

King's College Wimbledon

Haberdashers' Aske

Emmanuel School

Oundle School

The Perse School

Manchester Grammar School

These are but a few of those available. More can be unearthed by surveying the web pages of other schools. Sometimes these are difficult to find and will require a certain amount of digging around on their website. Some top schools do not publish past papers as a matter of policy, for example, Westminster School, but internet research can unearth appropriate and comparable materials, many of which are free. It is important to note that past papers for City of London School and Latymer School do provide some answers/marking schemes to their grammar and comprehension tests, and also to their past papers in mathematics. In conclusion, the web is an invaluable resource for home-based materials but when dealing with maths especially, answers to the questions are not generally available.

Publications

English Key Stage 2 - Schofield and Simms - age graded.

The Nelson Series – English - age graded.

Junior English Hayden Richards (available with answers).

The New First Aid in English 2ⁿᵈ Edition Angus Maciver. Available with answer book. Maciver is packed with information and vocabulary, similes, antonyms, spelling lists etc.

The Bond Series for all areas of maths, English, verbal reasoning and non-verbal reasoning. This series has become, in many ways, a standard work for home tuition and ubiquitous and in its usage. Everyone uses these useful texts, which are age graded and contain answers. They are very useful training before approaching past papers. All papers such as this should eventually be given on a timed basis when accuracy is becoming quite good.

Concerning multiple choice, the Bond Series texts are useful in this area as they provide answers and only a very small percentage of published 11+ papers for English provide multiple choice answers. Answers to multiple choice English are important for speed of marking and clarity of explanation. (However, sometimes answers are not at all clear to the tutor/trainer and occasionally some of them are wrong, particularly with regard to maths!)

GL Assessment - The Official 11+ Practice Papers

These are handy resource packs which contain a range of papers: maths, English, Verbal and

Non-Verbal Reasoning. These are useful as they cover all the different facets of the 11+ examinations in one pack.

Eleven Plus Vocabulary Flash Cards: Eleven Plus Flash Cards Publishing 1ˢᵗ Edition 31 Dec 2014

Materials such as flash cards can be very valuable for learning vocabulary. Three to five words may be introduced on a weekly basis to be included in the writing or comprehension passage by the pupil. The effect of this is cumulative in terms of the pupil's range of language and can extend this range dramatically and almost imperceptibly over time.

Eats, Shoots and Leaves by Lynne Truss, Profile Books 2003

This is aimed at adults and is highly recommended for the parent who wants a good grounding or revision in English grammar. It is not really intended for children of this age but some of them may find parts of it useful.

For children who may be dyslexic:

Dyslexia Techniques by Esther de Burgh-Thomas;

visit website for further details: dyslexiatechniques.com

Other useful websites include:

www.elevenplusexams.co.uk

Contains much useful information

www.theschoolrun.com

Again a lot of useful information as well free and paid-for practice papers for all types of examinations for under 12s as well as general advice.

Most bookshops and on-line book retailers hold the various resources set out above or can be easily ordered. This list is, of course, not exhaustive but I am listing materials that I am familiar with and which are fit for purpose. Advice may be gleaned from such websites as 'Mumsnet' as to the requirements and vagaries of particular schools. Working to a high standard with good materials will yield good results. Some schools only provide specimen papers and parents will have to learn to research themselves as to what is available at the time of tutoring.

RECOMMENDED LIST OF CHILDREN'S CLASSICS

Alice in Wonderland	Lewis Carroll
The Secret Garden	Frances Hodgson Burnett
JungleBook/JustSo Stories	Rudyard Kipling
The Happy Prince	Oscar Wilde
King Solomon's Mines	Rider Haggard
Tom Sawyer	Mark Twain
White Fang/Call of the Wild	Jack London
Narnia Series	C S Lewis
William Series	Richmal Crompton

20000 Leagues Under the Sea/Rocket to the Moon	Jules Verne
The Time Machine	H G Wells
Treasure Island/Kidnapped	Robert Louis Stevenson
The Railway Children	E Nesbitt
Tom's Midnight Garden	Philippa Pearce
The Wind in the Willows	Kenneth Grahame
The Hobbit/ The Ring Series	J R R Tolkien
The Wizard of Oz	Frank Baum
A Christmas Carol/Oliver Twist	Charles Dickens
Little Women	Louisa May Alcott

Black Beauty	Anna Sewell
Anne of Green Gables	Lucy Montgomery
The Little House on the Prairie	Laura Ingalls Wilder
The Machine Gunners	Robert Westall
The Borrowers	Mary Norton
Heidi	Johanna Spyri
Matilda	Roald Dahl
Carrie's War	Nina Bawden
Robinson Crusoe	Daniel Defoe

This list is a guide and has been kept short. A few more "modern" works have been included.

CONCLUSION

If you follow the ideas and practices outlined in this guide, then pupils will naturally raise their grade. The 11+ is a difficult exam for many pupils and it is becoming more difficult all the time, due, no doubt, to the number of applications schools receive which increase year by year. City of London School, for example, cites one applicant for every 10 places on their website. In July 2017, 3000+ pupils sat for the first Latymer School exam (North London) for 192 places.

Therefore, in light of the above, the more "professional" parents are in their approach, the more likelihood of obtaining a place, although, of course, this cannot be guaranteed. Despite all the obvious drawbacks such as stress, finances and time, parents and pupils who take this approach, in my experience, are much more likely to succeed. Hard work and time spent on past papers is usually well rewarded.

Some pupils appear to be able to drift through the process and succeed with minimal effort, but these are increasingly in the minority, as the exam becomes ever more difficult. Similarly, parents who want their children to do well and have a more casual, laid back approach, and who think their children might as well "have a go", have children that are rarely accepted. This is not to say that their children do not have ability or intelligence, rather they are not properly prepared with the requisite technical skills. Slightly sophisticated grammar and expanded vocabulary and the use of literary devices can raise marks dramatically. In addition, excellent spelling and mastery of the times tables, paragraphing and clear handwriting are essential and combine to create success.

In most primary schools, even very good primary schools, pupils with ability are rarely pushed or extended in their work and the general standard is not conducive to prepare for the rigours of the 11+.

The short worked example passages give insight as to how comprehension questions should be addressed and the level of difficulty and the issues involved in training. I hope they prove to be of some value in assisting pupils who are endeavouring to achieve a place.

Never forget that if your child is unsuccessful in the examination, he or she will still have had a thorough grounding in the principles of English if you have followed this guide and this will stand in very good stead when going on to secondary school – your (and their) time has been well spent whatever the result.

I hope you will find this guide useful.

Stuart Riddle

London

August 2017

ABOUT THE AUTHOR

Stuart Riddle has been teaching for over 30 years, the last 10 of which have been as a private tutor. He has a degree in European Studies from the University of East Anglia and undertook further research in history gaining a Master of Letters post-graduate degree at Cambridge. He also has a Post-Graduate Certificate in Education.

He can be contacted at:
tutorstuart@gmail.com